REALLY
SERIOUS
LITERATURE

Gwendalynn Roebke's voice is forthright and unflinching. The speaker of these poems asks hard and searing questions of the self and of humanity.

"Can you scrub suffering from plasma?"...

"Why delude our/perceptions/hoping injury will/hurt less?"

"...if there were no taste to lying would you still indulge so often?"

These 26 "bruxist" poems gnaw as well as invite us toward "black holes" of knowing and not knowing, all the while nudging the reader out of stasis and reminding that "time has always been hesitant to love us."

I look forward to more work from this new writer.

Marcia Douglas, author of *The Marvellous Equations of the Dread*

A Bruxist Manifesto presents us Gwendalynn Roebke as an old soul taking new form. Journal entries that read as songs of the Earth. A graceful fuck you dancing ballet over our hearts. Prophecy at the mezcla of eastern and western philosophy. An ululation attempting to call in the absurd ego of humanity in a wet world facing fire. Roebkes prose grinds down any borders that try to dim this burning holler of sorrow and hope. This manifesto of unabashed truth ringing generations forwards and backward, sideways and slantways.

Brice Maiurro, Founding Editor, South Broadway Press

a bruxist manifesto

gwendalynn roebke

acknowledgements

I am not really sure how to write an acknowledgement page. Do I do a standard BIPOC poet move and praise ancestors without specifying which ones drown the others? I am never sure anymore...

Who I will thank, are my family, my professors, and the other BIPOC poets who have had such a profound influence on me.

I do not remember the dead as if they were not ever living, and so instead I will thank the living before they pass.

contents

lamentation
in an era of
ghosts:
cry out for the living as you would the dead, we
will get there on our own. a congregation of
hungry jubilation, darkness melded to light. time
has always been hesitant to love us as we dig our
nails in to stay.

I.
smoke / mist

pathogen passed between exhales, will we bear to
see what the sheddings of this reality leave
behind? cosmic soot occupying our wrinkled
smiles; an outer envelope of energy tears itself
away from frame, and we call this resilience. stare
at ourselves for being while becoming, while
surviving, all explosive celestial oddity. tune in to
what it takes to be   uncomfortable lessons in
human nova anatomy. can't be with breath beat
out, with breath tangled in lungs from disease.
fragile fire that leaves no damage, our spirits are
spectacles. yet, you will not spot us easily. follow
water, and there is a chance you ll understand our
emergence. signals in the stars and the rivers, lead
us to wherever we can dock without first being
unknown.

2.
blood / laughter

so i say, we are not meant to be well in this
world. transcendental, trauma takes up residence
in our veins.
it spills out in the Earth, watch the tongues eager
to tell other stories. can you scrub suffering from
plasma?

so i say, there is joy still. born from rage and
between battles. ululation at surrender. brutality is
refashioned into a joke.
mask misery in wit, see who chuckles without
reason and make a note. new strategic self
flagellation.

3.
wound / scar

livid memories awaken in air speckled with
cottonwood wool.
it snows in june with cold welcomed for keeping
scalding predispositions at bay.
concrete chilled, there are burns on people who
barely made it out. and those who didn t, are
buried.

when is it appropriate to declare a person
deceased. dead. no longer of this world?
is it so bad to say we are something other than
beings belonging to this place?
would you have the courtesy to kill us for show,
but leave us living were we to clap into existence
another universe?

there will be no names here. an endless scroll of
unattended hospital beds and vigils makes it
almost disingenuous.

it is injustice to speak up genocide like its casual
maybe its become it.
we will just say Black, and know there is an
executioner in the background. we will just say
Indigenous, and dream.

4.
body / voice

rotten under the skin, decay is best hidden using
perfumed oils. musk makes it all seem
sophisticated...
a neck is not supposed to bend like that.
a skeleton can not remain intact after a backward
swan dive off a balcony.
a community that has only stayed vibrant under
pressure because of each other cannot keep
distance easily.

when they pull a dancers corpse from the sea and
tell his people they couldn t save him earlier
how badly did they want for his kind to drown?
flood a holy land with violence to clean history.
there are public massacres every morning news
cycle and is it cruel to want this to bind us
now that everyone fears losing breath, will we
want to learn how to store air together in our
throats?

watch reverberations from footsteps outside
shake fluid in an IV. doctors have deemed this
necessary care.
bombs are still on target. there will be casualties
called mistakes...remember it is all intentional.
sound each infraction of self out loud. let it be
heard, waves must travel through something.
we are the medium. even when a message is
scattered from shaken mouths, it can hold
wisdom.

let this be a fuck you. we are not bold, just tired,
and what better lullaby than rebellion.
each awakening is more salient than the next. a
second storm of disease will not tuck us in.
we haven t trusted your gifts for a long time. we
have stories of those who steal oil off skin and
steal children.
oral histories of loss speak to the void and you
will find it full, ready to bloom.

5.
rebirth / forgetting

i have no forgiveness.
wrenching likeness from an IG post at 1 in the
morning. counting how many were left behind.
whispering a prayer for each viewing. due
diligence in sending silent condolences.
wicked be the alters unadorned with the words of
the mourned. omitting makes a lifetime a
consumable object.
i have no forgiveness.

directions arent received in a culture of rugged
individuality without a war.
you need the visuals of morgues overflowing.
cadavers kept in containers on the street.
theres a love for avoidable tragedy so long as it
can entertain the untouched.
apologies, it is not us   it is that looming past.
lets walk as if you are not injured, and as if the
injury is not related to the knife in my hand.

if we draw another punch,will we be called weak
or merciful? the bell is rung echoing out defeat.
where is disrest revolution and where is it a
nuisance it's not as romantic when it arrives on
your own conscience.
take a baton to the ribcage. scream justice will not
see you fall. but it will if it is law masquerading as
justice.
so, the ask is one not of righteousness but need.
because the basic steps couldn t be followed
before.
another round is on, there is no time to worry
about sportsmanship. it s a brawl , now the rigging
is up.

repeat after me, i am more than the ancestors
who survived because they made sure others
didn t ...
it is naive to fantasize of lineages unscathed by
treachery. those to whom you pray musn t be
sacred.

but do not make mortal idol. bare teeth , blot
out names, you can kick out abusers even if
they re kin.
don t be sorry.
i mean it. dont, be , sorry.

i have no forgiveness.
portraits of the greater good will not console me.
you have not shown me that you know how to
mend me or my people.
so what good is this. i know medicine is bitter.
this, however, is carcinogenic and you ve tried to
cover it in sugar.
the tally will not continue if we have our way.
there will be rest not disturbed with flash bangs
or bloody heaving.
a snap so long it was confused for us being
bendable. i assure you we aren t.
we have no forgiveness... kneel.

walk too upright and they ll slide more on your
shoulders:
born to a Black ballerina i've seen my mother
fight gravity

thump out beats on my chest
out comes 4 ghosts and a djinn

you were supposed to be a dancer

walk tip toe made a foot taller
pool water in your collarbones
all while pinning limbs to air

but you re here

summoning spirits
 making music on your flesh

an iraqi woman asks me where my parents are
from
offers me tea as she inspects the nape of my
neck
i would show her the map of my curls
however i am afraid she will no longer consider
me kin

smiling my south sudanese coworker and i leave
without tea and without me telling her

i was supposed to be a dancer

would i tell a room with 3 refugees
my mother wanted something so frivolous for
me...

my teacher, took me aside when i said i wanted
to quit
told me i had the look
forlorn, lanky, charismatic beauty

i ve grown into reluctantly
calluses dominant the tips of my toes

go on point in the kitchen
performing alone

burning
I skipped out on destiny

__the meek are ready for their inheritance:__
go to mars, we re taking Earth and the guillotine
is eager to see you off

whittled hole in atmosphere
with our
artificial object obsession

we re missing breath
maybe that s why we re so
lightheaded

can t think right
so we re out here
cannibalizing our
caretaker
heaving
having torn sky

foolish for believing the lesion will heal
fully

heaven doesn t trust us anymore

think we need to cauterize the horizon
seal off dawn till we re
worthy

stars that birthed us click

their tongues
as our own Sun
sucks its teeth
embarrassed
punishment pending
red curtain coming sooner
courtesy of our own hubris

having us cocky enough to
cast stones

not knowing
they're the same ones
that will be used
to sink us

amor, habibti, lieber
do not pay for a plot to bury me, your memories
will do

i set the drinking water
on fire
it was fucking filthy

you re
welcome
for my impulsive
indiscretion

manic savior
i ve got a heathen's
knack
for tilling land
and taking prisoners
 to convert

lovers

with soft hands
set to undo knots around the heart
when they take themselves
free
from anything not scented by Sod

i've practiced which herbs

will bring me victory
bottled them
 to bless my friends

ginger is said to evoke
firey protection
here s hoping the root
drying on my shelf
isn t for
nothing

my mom casually told me i was at risk for
schizophrenia
i was 10 and i've carried a pocket knife for the
shadows ever since

embalm bodies instead of
bombing them
can we give nothing back
to the Earth?
formaldehyde may be better
than shrapnel
each ugly in their
respective insidiousness

intimate disembowelment
lets dissect the ways
we know each other
interrogate human ego
aching to find a clear motive
 for all this

the smell leaves stains on
ceilings
none of the neighbors knock
in an apartment complex with
 several hundred
decomposition goes on uninterrupted

im the worst worshipper i know
nearly choked to death in a mega church
on a mint given to me by a stranger
12 years almost wasted in 1 minute

torrential storms skulk over skylines
please, turn off all the lights

we can sit here
 praying
or just watch all this
become

blurry

moonscapes for maps:
i learned baghdad was the intellectual capital of
the muslim world for a while and know now why
the west has tried to scrape it from the earth

you cannot be empty
for how full a place this is
no people carry nothingness
 inside

heard them shouting for you...
resonance in your entrails
gut on fire with the instinct fly

they've linked arms to march
summon a riot
 as is memory wanting to do

have you read the story
of the child who went to
war for a day
and came back a king...

such ramblings are story for a reason
why fight for a kingdom
there is a heaven above us

owned by no hands
all the lovelier left out

but you better get to the sky
on sunny days they make villages
into myth

you ve been needed
that stomach ache won t wane
until you listen

mud people:
cryptids are more abundant than you think, and
we want our keeper well

called
We
Dirt
so it became us
The Dirt
grew Earth s lungs
elated
when you survive something
meant
to kill you
you will become a monster
called us Dirt
and themselves
human
why would We want to
 be known
in the same name
say Dirt
the antithesis other
monster
breathed the world

glory be as it is:
closet as a keeper , maybe it is cowardice. but you
only say our names when you need to signal
virtue and I won t die for your feed.

wash the piercing in salt
dangling from your ear
a new pendant
wear a warped shell casing

give me the sterile promise
of revolt

there are two love poems i have memorized
one in spanish
to all of mankind
one in english
a drowning ballad of sirup

remember love justified romantic nationalisms
love this land you ll skin for it
love this woman you ll kill her for it
love your body you ll break it for it

i m sorry i wanted more than this
if i wasn t so hungry i d have a quiet stomach
and wouldn t disturb lecture with my growling

they ll never thank you when you remove a
tyrant's head
from their shoulders
not when they are the tyrant

so don t expect applause
but be ready to run

let s be interesting

talk of crumbling dynasties
dictators setting forests alight

provocative in caring just enough

drinks and a smile
will you be at the protest or the vigil?
the union meeting or the funeral?

here s the edge

catty, queer, ready to fight
 unless
 the fight is anything other than a love poem
requires an arm not a tattoo gun and a new
earring

i m not brave enough to be butch anymore

since i was threatened with a fucking
i mean a fixing

i loved this body so i broke it to save it
it
 the flesh,
me the imp loving it wrong by calling it cage,
it beast

cheers to the memorization of the steps to
liberation
adorned and unarmed

ghandi and good aren t synonymous:
*its not divisive. when people are antiblack peace
is a smoke screen.*

disjointed
radicalism
falls

omits in favor of
rose laden memories
caskets as decoration

stories as myth

sure
joy is a blade
but dug into the wrong rib cage
misnomer

revolution in regress

roses encased in glass:
we were too eager, the little prince knew this

i have been keeping a garden
in small terracotta pots
there i ve let my heart grow again
from seed
over ambitious the basil
chokes one another
bends over and dies
i must practice
reaching for sunlight and sipping water
press lips to leaves
play melancholy ballads
in seven different languages
i want sustenance in sorrow
spanning across the globe
croon to them in only 2 tongues
let them know my voice
my heart, i ll tend to you twice a day
tell you stories of rotten roots
of the others buried behind my memories
insufferable heat , sweating in sub zero
temperatures
i will watch you
moon flower and lemon balm
break the soil
i ve waited too long for my own reunion

i get weird when i ride airplanes:
*i project my fever for change on them hoping we
won t crash*

stale prayers spat to keep us airborne

machines doing work spanning continents
pregnant, with the belongings
the baggage
of one hundred plus passengers

it s just physics

thrust, momentum, gauging pressure
we may pop, pulled from stratosphere
scattered across horizon

it took decades to learn
lift

we ll get there
baggage and all

ACAB for a new age:
complacency is complicity

want us
pinned hands
in prayer

so we
kill flies
applauding
always jubilant
in a sweltering summer

all
holy death
tiny offering

cookout so hot
hell yawned, awakened , opened

exoskeletons emptied from clammy palms into
Earth
Black bodies emptied from joyous park gathering
into
Earth

clap rattle echo
of a lost heartbeat

clap rattle echo
of a public secret genocide

Life's a Stage.

_Is the Production a Tragedy or a Rock Opera? It
doesn't matter. The hero still dies._

scene
crying on set?
there s a corner for that

with how many runs
there are
 in your
 voice
one would think you re
worn ragged
by now

will you sing?
unused
what good
is music

why must everything find usage...

use for what?

we need an anthem

a Messiah

to measure how far we ll go
forgetting lines and
 letting
limelight shine on folx unworthy

you don t have the temperment
to drag a
cross
 across the sky

nor
 a people through the
 realms of the dead

act over

cover your face for shame
veil of sharp notes struck to dissuade
destiny

partial credit for partial feelings:
lets smear our longing on bread

1000 embraces
 away from you

why can t we measure more things
in increments of affection

timekeeping keen
to tilt
instances
into
f o r e v e r

preserve
the now
 in
saccharide sanctuary

honey
will heal
will hold

as it always has

*i only learned to wear a seatbelt when i slammed
into a headrest and ruined my smile*

i do not pretend
a broken arm
is a wing

why delude our
perceptions
hoping injury will
hurt less?

some things need
to be seen
broken
to be fixed

pain is supposed to be a precursor
to healing

we shouldn t
 hurt ourselves
to heal

just accept
not everything must be
rewritten

damage

done
 is
damage

it is not always an
opportunity to start
anew

the limb
will heal
perhaps less agile than before

the heart
will continue on
warier than its first love

duck and cover:

*continual bombardment is not a time to rebuild
we are painted in bruises and hear echoes of loss.
from cultures founded in survival, how do we get
past this?*

supposed to be
bomb proof

with our
lead bones
bunker bodies

fit,
for emotional
fallout

made lethal

when what
saved us
made us

sick

cancerous
self preservation
of the too strong
strong people

secluded
waiting
for the hidden hurt s
 resurfacing

struggle lurking

we ve acclimated
to internal guerrilla combat

gestation:
when Black and Brown Bellies swell we get ready
for wakes. if we make it through delivery there
will be weeping either way.

i was born from a wound that
would not close

would you not name a womb this way?

how it
bleeds
and
bleeds

bearing the infection of
loss
only
loss

as it gives the world
another being
to lose

faul tongues translate gift two ways :
poisonous sloth, growing nimble in languages
means giving up presents.

wear white
in
war

tribute
to its ultimate disciples

some
recognize it submission
but meaning
is fluid

as is the body
tipped over
staining history
burgundy

we ll find wounds easier this way
masquerading as doves
dirtied
in
dissent/descent

whether or not our sores are
dressed

doesn t concern
the sea

for now here is the title.

still I cannot let the poem begin without trying to
explain my soul and the stitches there. i want to
do my best to say the Earth fell from under
millions of people with different skins before and
they survived somehow so ill start the poem
and try not to vilify those who ought to be
organizing just please i cannot name a poem
without attempting to infuse my heart

doomsday clock
is at fewer
than 3 minutes to midnight

meaning
the current world is

Closing

3
 microwave minutes

you can make a
maruchan ramen in that time

ingest enough sodium to
 stop
 a heart

i stole that line

all is fair in
 love and apocalypse

and the person who wrote the line
didn t love me

and the world of some humans misplaced itch for
domination seems
to be drawing shut

so i will steal what i like

poetry can only be so kind

what will i do?
paint a bullet
write a war cry

if every artist picked up a weapon
not words
would we be closer to ending this

if every academic learned to heal
not talk
could the clock tick back a couple hours

describe the end to me

and you ll see history has been
gracious
in giving us precursors

a bubble bath won't clean you of your self
loathing becky:
capitalism will call on you to purchase your own
love and pretend scented candles can undo the
damage of epigenetic trauma.

words worn
threadbare

we ought to stop cloaking our
doubt
in garments so thin as
performative affection

claim yourself
— without sound
be a scream unuttered

there exist
more durable praises
stitched in our skin

potent
were you to assert it
yours

you can only have so many pastors in a family:
any more than 2 and i promise you, you'll be
eaten by sanctity

i wash my skin in
summer winds

its been 13 rotations since i
began
to know breathlessness

i learned to wiggle my ears
from a man
 who died
and preached
of God

john henry proportions
mountain made a wisp

his flock sang his way to the chariot
who knew sheep could keep a tune?

they have tried to make
sensitive
to mean
breakable

and

they push
till

people snap
violent
people snap
self preservation
people snap
unfeeling

delicate people
are
seen as
so
malleable...

for a while i kept a
 toad as a pet

cupped my hands
 and felt each tremor
of its attempted escape
should i have pressed my palms together
since gentle is just pressure unapplied?

force of knees
 reconnecting with turf
 after each jump

i can carry a skinned shoulder
and people
70 pounds more
my weight
without
misstepping

when the sun's out
my chain rubs raw
the memory of its prior
 owner
who
stood soft as each sibling
 passed her

i am stamped into time
the mountain side is on fire
we cannot run today
 as the smoke sticks
 to our sweat

but i m cleaned
by the breeze
lukewarm
ashen shower

jiggling my jaw
between sprints
as i was

taught

to call in or call out:
depends, how many bodies did their words leave
in their rise

this diet of
salt and tea
has me dehydrated

there s more to talking
than this

my tongue is not as nimble
as i'd like it
crude and confrontational

when i spit in another language
its brutish
like i m trying to tear down
the ceiling
or something

i m all ribs
bruised smile and pulsing aura
i know enough of what i need to
to say
i m tired
We re tired
and there are going to be changes

god is dead;
suicide calls for us all i guess
cheeky sure, though i have a beef with the god in
my nanas prayers. she says we were chosen for
this punishment and will reap the reward of
drowned flesh, but i'd rather avenge my kin with
an emptied sea and an admission of wrongs
between our celebrations....

just heat and ineffable ecstasy
sway of brazen hips and untethered hearts

growling stomachs filled with ardor,
their roar rewriting the beat blowing out of
oversized speakers.

small talk and long embraces...

no time for anything but this lost moment;

these occasions
 when the world allowed lovers to lean in close,
offering each other breath and body without the
threat of ends

but it all ends,
it must.

fading,
feelings scatter into the immenseness of
forgettery.

holy has forgotten how to heal,
misplaced its place in this modern depravity .

the bass brings the partition to their chattering
knees,
needing something to believe in;

this beat, these bodies, those burning desires

something , more than what comes in a night
and leaves by the mornings fresh faced fear to be
but a child without a god

or,
a god without children...

though
these carefree kids be their own kind of god.

a new type,
of contemporary cutthroat deities whose deaths
seem nothing but the birth of new stars .

shimmering, dead things decorate the heavens
the remnants of remembered lost moments!

shards of new gods gotten before their time.

nietzsche knows nothing of the burn of this
modern man of god!

priests of the after party,
saints of the kick back,
disciples of drug use and loose kisses

god is dead!
the wake continues...

el tesoro de Carne Negra /
the treasure of Black Flesh

instead of heads
it ll be hands
woven around my waist
pierced at the wrist
threaded through hemp rope
dyed
violet

i ll make wine
of a man
beneath my feet
prostrated to appease me

get drunk on purging
wrath
annebrieted protector
still, clear in path
a chorus of trampled cowards
who thought wrongly the woozyness of
vision
would deter sighted vengeance

you cannot be trusted
with the gift of us
blotted out the sun
unhindered expanses of our

untreated follicle

cut circulation
wrapped tight
 on divisions to digits

we said to decolonize chaos
and thank us for its delivery
supposed disorder
is the blessing
 revered method

the water you wash with
is from our mouths
attending to incantations
bes unbothered by your slander
ignorant to our maintenance
of this plane of experience

good sandalwood does not come out of
the pores after one shower:
it marks you, with a spiced musk, so you
can cleave through the rank untruths

picking out pebbles from an impact
abrasion
it s difficult to fix grip on slick earth under
the dermis remove what may find refuge
in you.
were we smashed against the world, and
fixed ourselves with gold to finally be
valuable?

kintsugi applied to emoting flesh.
vulnerable unlike ceramic because the
cracks aren t always sealable...
or was it with informed malice that we
were shattered to expose the ore within
us?

know, if you re doing what I think you re
doing when you say its prayer;
let every herb you burn without wisdom
cause illness. wastefulness of a holy not
yours bind you to your misery all the
more as you threaten the existence of
plants named sacred by other tongues.

i ask, if there were no taste to lying would
you still indulge so often?

let the stone live with you, be you.
directions back to the fall.
mined from an error, tripping over how
to proceed coveted.

Joya:
refitted for my mouth, i keep crossroads

there s only one of them i keep with me.
they ve got rusty syllables for a name   and they're
enough of me to never ask that i stumble through
saying it.

i could sit here and write what was requested.
a poem that breaks the skin. floral, folding into
hymn, a harness , so you can keep yourself here...

it s the home whose residents had fangs surface
on the valves of their aortas;
yowling with each compression, it's what happens
when a heart must be protected in a body
brought out of the badlands.

i tend to use of instead of from; i am not from a
place i am of a People who ripped down the sky
of their own creation. fuck your love if it s docile,
quiet won t keep clever though you hope it might.

regression

the kept jewel in my ear, we rest in mulch,
watching a criss cross wire fence collect tumble
weeds.
on monday, we will move from the mulch to the
tire swing.
 i will get a bloody nose,
a child of leaky head and runny thoughts,
and will make no effort to keep my shirt clean.

from this, I will take the wisdom to only wear
Black.
to muffle the sound of my chest.
to press flowers between my favorite stanzas, and
never speak our shared name.

bruxism:

when sleeping there are those of us who
gnaw enamel stress induced hunger for
our own bloody gums hoping this meal of
the self will mean there's nothing left for
others to take. nothing is not absence; as
celestial anomalies aren t impossible, just
difficult to make human.

5.
mindful bites / black hole

let s end as we started. format seems to matter.
i ve a sprawling voice, which makes sense for a
love of entropy.
5 sections, each a finger for a palm. embellish
digits with rings and hangnails.
two hands, press close for the poem. ugly but
covered in the equivalent of precious metals using
slick words.
as they say, two divine palms pressed applause
for the beginning.
how off beat were they? that this were all to
happen? on the 1 and 3, it shows.

bad breath can be a sign of a souring mouth.
it is pressure put on an old filling that escorts me
to the dentist.

i am fitted for a mouth guard. told to watch when
i clench my jaw. to try and be better.
 brushing teeth removes plaque not anxiety. if
anything, the more anxious you are the more you
brush
because you can fix it right? hard work 2 times a
day. diligence and mindfulness. not the root, it
promotes corrosion.

again, pressure, is, e v e r y t h i n g.
the stars, societal upheaval, folding over of gas
clouds to create new fusion.
we need this to buckle, but in the right places.
otherwise you get stray elements and an unborn
coup.
it is needed for me to recognize i am destroying
myself in silence. and night reminds me of this.
i wake up and cannot eat on one side. i speak
slanted for a week.

but i also want to get to the impossibility of this
all. here in the most perfect of possible worlds .
i am caught on the concept of a kerr newman
black hole. charged, and rotational.
it opens up the flirtation of alternate worlds.
parallel dimensions and a tubular singularity.
 my professor is quick to tell us that in reality no
such thing is capable of existing.
friction,is the foe of this dream.

i am dying in the embrace of a dream.unspecified.
know how the grinding of peoples brings heat.
how heat, is both good and bad in change and
inaction.
when we rub against each other trying to make
movements, its like thick thighs in jeans in
summer
well bust the seams of something and chaffing
will ensue. we never fit them anyway but well
mourn their loss.
even when it makes no sense well be sad. though
we can hope the pain subsides as something
different comes.

4.
gold / collapse

depreciation in value is why things tend to fall. in
human hands. empires and the like.
we lose interest, or lose the need to keep things.
holding is a difficult task. being kept is easy.
though, there are a few things that just are
we pay in the things that are with little attention
to why.

whys are unnerving. which may explain the
sentiment that those who pursue them are
aggravating people.
there s a reason white, cis , heterosexual men rule
philosophy, the domain of whys.
they think their opinions matter the most their
answers and methods for grappling whys
somehow stronger.
they re not. but what use is it to critique the
shutters of an unstable house when you could just
burn it.

taking up all the air with their promises of perfect
argumentation. it s premeditated.

flame can t ignite without oxygen. and they know
this. they is all who take shelter in a system, keep
pace.
i think it's silly to be apologetic when you smash
what was meant to subjugate you.
harm is not in the eye of the beholder. my people
will be called violent when we ask to be seen.

my people is loaded i will admit. i look like
everyone who s ever been brought to dust.
when i am yelled at next to mohammed, the man
looks at me to say fuck Palestine, i m pro
semitic
i laughed. i prefer tailored racism. if he d spoken
about water and nooses, cops and reservations,
then he d get me.
he is of the people after whom i name the holes in
my teeth. he is a thought that leads to locked
molars and fillings.

3.
deep clean / nebula

here is where i should quote hafiz, or neruda, or
rumi on love. how we forget their poems of the
people.
but i have chosen to quote silence. a faceless
miracle of pause.
it would be poetic to say i have chosen silence
because you don t read it. but you should, fair
weather friend.

here is where i regain composure. femmes
outspoken discomfort will be branded as agitation
and i can t have that.
covered in the handprints of other people s
pleasure; touch is a dangerous thing to bestow
upon the feral.
i was indoctrinated into knowing a sand colored
body as a conflict zone. lucky, to get out with a
monument left.

here is where i come to look at the beautiful
things destruction can grow. but lets be careful,
colonizers are eagerly listening.
you know, all the pictures we have of deep space
are artists renderings. their imaginations applied
over lightyears.
every rainbow after an explosion of loose stardust
is their dream. i'm jealous, they may sleep with
unground canines.

2.
numbing / supernova

what is right to share with others? belongs
enough to me and not my family. its not to be
elusive, or so i say
there is a need for me to write about the great
grandmother who was caught one night on the
railroad tracks with her child.

my grandmother, in her mother's hands, was set
to die. and the need to make things pretty tells
me to say there were stars out.
too Black, too Brown, too damaged by the world
she ended in a mental hospital. her husband
remarried.only my name visited.

caries / red giant

am i not like justice? inconvenient , in how i need
to be loved.
should i tell you about the map of scars on my
back? after the phase of midnight snacks made
out of my mouth waned, i moved on to digging
red out of myself. a replacement coping strategy,
giving myself small craters because to the dentist
that was better by what was concealed. in my
fingernails there is my own flesh. in
absentmindedness i undo my spine. i can hold all
this i swear. fingers knotting jynx behind me.
there are stars inked on my ribs now, and i use
them to navigate my way home.we have come to
the end at the beginning. inverted and clapping at
an odd tempo, inner ridges smoothed. there are 2
defining happenings, a bang and the wandering
into a small whiteness. eternity is one. but
eternity isn t everything.

Gwendalynn is Black/multiracial, gender non conforming, they/them just doing their best to exist. They write and perform poems that try their damndest to have meaning... but really thats for other people to determine and has been subjective bearing to how good a poem is. Are they a poet? Debatable. Really they just want to write interesting things and design their own tattoos.

CPSIA information can be obtained
at www.ICGtesting.com
Printed in the USA
BVHW031614191221
624255BV00002BA/135